The Dual Sides

of

My Gemini Mind

LaRhonda N. Felton

LaRhonda N. Felton

The Dual Sides of My Gemini Mind

Copyright © 2019 by LaRhonda N. Felton.

All rights reserved.

Each poem included in this compilation is based on the author's original idea or concept. No part of this original work may be reproduced in any way without permission from the author, except by a reviewer. For interviews or any inquiries pertaining to the content of this publication, please contact the author and/or publisher.

Email: LaRhondaNFelton@gmail.com
Facebook.com/AuthorLaRhondaNFelton
Instagram: @Author_LaRhondaNFelton

Edited, Formatted, Published via *iWrite4orU*
www.iWrite4orU.com
Cover Image: iStock Photo
ISBN: 978-0-9998842-6-3
LCCN: 2019906964

Printed in the United States of America

LaRhonda N. Felton

Reviews for In The Meantime

"Do yourself a favor and buy this for you and your significant other to read in bed together, or better yet send excerpts to your lover in a text while you're apart. Give credit to the author though…"

"This book was phenomenal. There were so many poems that I could relate to at this time in my life. It takes you on emotional rollercoaster that we as women have gone through at some point in our lives!"

"The roller coaster of emotions that the book takes you on is incredible. Loved the fact that you can always find a way to relate to each poem."

"A must-read book! It's captivating from the beginning to the end… You can't just read it once! Set the mood and let your mind go places you haven't gone before."

"…an erotic book of poems that will have you fanning if you don't have anyone to put out the fire."

"It's not just a page-turner, but it's a fire starter, and it's sure to excite the senses, tickle the fancies, and quench the thirsts…"

Available where all books are sold.

The Dual Sides of My Gemini Mind

Dedication

This is my second book and the number two represents my life number. Therefore, it seemed only natural that this book is dedicated to the woman that gave me life: My mom, Phyllis Felton. Mom, with all my heart, thank you. You have always encouraged and supported me being me. The fact that you have always had an open door that allowed me to express my feelings and experiences with no judgment has been priceless in my life. I am the woman I am today because of your nurturing & never hovering. I couldn't have done any of this without your unwavering love and support. Here's to you, Mom, and our B&B surrounded by white sands and turquoise water.

With all my love, your Gemini. Xoxo

To my Lord and Savior Jesus Christ, I thank you. Thank you somehow seems inadequate for the blessing of life and expression you have bestowed upon me. In December 2016 when I prayed and asked You to reveal the gift You wanted me to use immediately, the words began to pour through me at an alarming rate that baffles me. I am able to share feelings and emotions that we all experience as humans. My debt to you could never be repaid. I am humbled and eternally grateful.

Melissa Felton-Henderson, thank you my sissy, my number one fan and beta reader. You're one of my biggest supporters and cheerleaders. You believe in me when I don't believe in myself. I thank you from the bottom of my heart.

My brother, Lindsey 'Scooter' Felton. Thank you. I love you. I only have to say the word and you're there. You push me without ever knowing that you do. Thanks to my BIL, Derrick Henderson Sr., nephew Derrick 'DJ' Henderson, niece Michaela Henderson. I love you all and thanks very much for your love and support.

I must extend a special thank you to two people I love dearly, JoAnne McGriff-Hillord and Torrence Smith. You both made my first book a personal success. My love and eternal gratitude to you both.

My Meeting of The Minds Book Club sisters, Janaver Wooden, Toni Cash and Joye Powell. Thank you ladies for your constant encouragement and unwavering support. We are 15+ years strong in this

LaRhonda N. Felton

book club game. I couldn't imagine doing this with any other group. I love each one of you. Thank you. #HappyReading

My Editor and Publisher, Liltera R. Williams. I thank you from the bottom of my heart my sister. You push me to dig deeper when necessary. I am very grateful to you and looking forward to our projects in the future.

Special thanks to Etrec J. White and Rudolph Henderson. I truly appreciate your support.

My readers, your feedback and support means the world to me. It's very humbling when you take the time to leave a review or to let me know the enjoyment you receive when reading my life's passion. Thank you Monica Coleman, Ethelene Walker, Bennie Cummings. Jamise Barnett, LaTanya Carter and Kwatishea Dorsey. Thanks also goes to Vanessa French-Elerby, Vanessa Lang, Detrice Jackson, Regina Kohn and Sip & Flip Book Club.

I pray that you smile, cry and laugh along with me as you travel through The Dual Sides of My Gemini Mind.

Xoxo

LaRhonda N. Felton

Table of Contents

Sex	9
Denied	13
After Rush Hour	15
Behavioral Differences	19
Impatient	23
Heartbreak	29
Mind Made Up	33
Bedroom Shenanigans	37
Pendulum	41
Forewarned	43
Purple	47
Who Is He?	51
In His Arms	53
Ain't It Funny?	57
Sex Scene Pt II	59
Unplugged	63
Awakened	65
Emotionally Unavailable	67
Side Pieces	69
Long Distance	71
He Is Home	73
Too Late	75
Bad Idea	79
Needing More	83
Love All Over	85
Brokenhearted	87
Levels	93

Privileges Revoked	*95*
Deeper	*99*
Follow My Heart	*103*
Us	*105*
Soulmate	*107*
Second Thoughts	*109*
His & Hers	*113*
His Breaking Point	*115*
Untrustworthy	*119*
Quiet as Kept	*121*
Killing the Vibe	*125*
Your Worst Nightmare	*127*
Historically Speaking	*129*
On the Edge	*133*
Indica	*135*
Doubt	*137*
Time's Up	*139*
Got to be More Careful	*141*
Prioritize	*149*
Slow Dance	*151*
His Boys	*153*
Girls' Night Out	*161*
Gemini	*163*

The Dual Sides of My Gemini Mind

Sex

Gripping

Tightly

Gushing

Nightly

Hard

Strong

Thick

Long

Meet up

Beat up

Clean up

For the re-up

Touching

Squeezing

Licking

Pleasing

In the bed

On the couch

In the car

At your house

LaRhonda N. Felton

My breasts
Your chest
Moaning loudly
Oh, you're blessed

You're amazing
Giving head
Making me cum
Shaking legs
Sucking you deeply
Position sixty-nine
You nut hard
Saying you're mine

Sweat pouring
It's been too long
Next position
Prone bone
You're in deep
Hitting my G
Slapping my ass
"Mmm, baby please"

Slippery wet

The Dual Sides of My Gemini Mind

Noisy love-making

Tapping out

Bodies quaking

Exhausted, tired

Sleep is bound

Energizing ourselves

For the next round

LaRhonda N. Felton

The Dual Sides of My Gemini Mind

Denied

I said I needed you
And you never replied
I don't need someone often
But when I needed you, I was denied

I didn't press the issue
We even talked the next day
You told me you were there for a friend
Even stayed up late
Up late for a *friend*?

You say you love me
Yet, you show no concern
When I'm struggling
Your actions spoke volumes
Very loud and clear
That I'm not even rated *friend*
I'm wasting my time here

You've done wonders for my creativity
With all the pain you've caused
And taught me a valuable lesson

LaRhonda N. Felton

I need to step back and pause
You can't put my love on a shelf
And take it down at your convenience
I need love on a daily
One that's reciprocal and seamless

Thanks for the heads up
And being there for your real *friend*
For dismissing the fact that I needed you
And clearing my confusion in the end

The Dual Sides of My Gemini Mind

After Rush Hour

He comes through the door
Staring right at me
I look up at him
And feel a bolt of electricity

He kisses me deeply
With his tongue in my mouth
My body quickly responds
I'm puddling down south

We go to the bedroom
Since we need more space
We shed clothes so fast
They're all over the place

He pushes me on the bed
Gives my ass a hard smack
Then he pulls me up
And licks my pussy from the back

He's gripping my hips
His tongue in the right place

LaRhonda N. Felton

I don't hold back
I cum all over his face
That doesn't stop him
He loves to make me weak
He knows my body
And how to put me to sleep
He flips me over
Onto my back
His face still in my pussy
I'm under attack

He's using his fingers
Along with his tongue
I grip his head tighter
And once again I cum

He looks at me
As his face glistens
I beg him to stop
But he never listens

My heart is racing
As he plays with my nipples
He wants me to tap out

The Dual Sides of My Gemini Mind

It's that plain and simple

I cum for the third time
As my body shudders
I know I can't move
My legs feel like rubber

He comes up and smiles
Looks me right in my eyes
He says, "I told you when I got home
Your ass was mine"

LaRhonda N. Felton

The Dual Sides of My Gemini Mind

Behavioral Differences

Men always ask, *how did you know?*
When lies are no longer their savior
Blaming it on women's intuition
When all the time, it's their own behavior

His attitude changed
And he no longer made time
Stringing me along
And claiming to be all mine

Everything is different
Suddenly, you're always in a rush
And the minute I ask you about it
You're telling me to hush

And this time, I will
After all, it's mere speculation
I have no concrete proof
This inquisition, you've escaped it

Does that stop you?
Not at all, you're feeling like *the* man

LaRhonda N. Felton

Although you slow down
You push forward with your plans

And in that one simple moment
Just when you thought you were safe
Your entire life
Explodes in your face
All the lies you've told
Come crashing down
And the respect I had for you
Is nowhere to be found

Because when I gave you the chance
To tell your truth and come clean
You looked at me as if I were crazy
My feelings didn't mean a damn thing

Now you expect forgiveness
Wanting me to take pity
When you lied and cheated
Where is your accountability?

Dog a damn good woman
To run around being a hoe

The Dual Sides of My Gemini Mind

You must be out of your damn mind
To think I would let this go

I loved you, but you failed me
And truth be told
I have more trust in pots of gold
At the end of the rainbow

One thing about my intuition
It has never ever lied
You, on the other hand,
Couldn't be honest if you tried

LaRhonda N. Felton

Impatient

We were lying in bed
Finishing a book
His dick poking me
My sleep bra already unhooked

"Baby, how many more pages?
I want you so bad"
I said, "I can tell
With the way you keep rubbing my ass"
He laughed and said
"You need to take these off"
As he grabbed and pulled
At the panties he just bought

I put the book down
And crawled to the foot of the bed
I watched his expression as I
Slowly slid them down my legs

He's watching me
And licking his lips
He says, "come here baby"

LaRhonda N. Felton

As I swing my hips

I get back in bed
He's already naked
He smells so damn good
I can barely take it

We begin kissing
And touching
Getting super aroused
Moaning and sucking

We couldn't blame the book
This was our norm
The mere thought of each other
Brought fire to our loins

He's sucking my tongue
His lips soft and juicy
He makes sure I cum at least once
Before he's sliding into me

But tonight will be different
I have other plans in mind

The Dual Sides of My Gemini Mind

And he's going to beg for mercy
While I take my time

He's on his back
I remove his hands from my ass
And before he can move again
He hears the closing of the clasp

Handcuffed, tightly
The blindfold is next
He says, "baby you're playing dirty"
As I slowly lick his chest

I make my way down
Blowing hot air as I lick
I watch his expression
As I firmly grab his dick

I lick and suck him
Mouth full of spit
He's as hard as granite
As he says "baby, oh shit"

I know what I'm doing

LaRhonda N. Felton

And he's feeling it
I will take him to the brink
And push him past his limit

He wants to watch as I suck
He's a very visual creature
And I love his sex faces
Every single feature

I suck him lovingly
With my ass in the air
Too bad he's handcuffed
He loves playing in my hair

Ten minutes of head
And he's losing his mind
Just when he's on the verge
I know it's the perfect time

I remove the blindfold and cuffs
And prepare to ride
I push him back further
And slide him deep inside

The Dual Sides of My Gemini Mind

Gripping upon entry
He can finally grab my butt
I shudder from the feeling
As he strokes and fills me up

He says, "baby you're in trouble"
As I ride, I ask him why
I say, "I owed you one, remember?
And your payback came tonight"

I stick my tongue in his mouth
That always shuts him up
We compete sexually
Cause we both love to fuck
He's tapping out first
As I clench my walls
I lean back slightly
And grip his balls

That's it right there
The face I wanted to see
He's nuttin' hard
Face full of ecstasy

Heartbreak

So, he cheated
And kept coming around
Had me looking like the fool
All around town

He explained how he cooked
And she decided to stay
I told him like most dogs do
When you take pity on a stray

He kept insisting
That he loved me
I guess he didn't care
That I'd given him my virginity

So, my love for him
Couldn't be measured
Being my first
He was hard not to treasure

But I had to get over it
Play it very cool

LaRhonda N. Felton

Or keep longing for him
Continuing to play the fool

That wasn't me
And I would never be her for him
He needed to realize
I was the priceless gem
Not just some random
He found on the street
That I am one of a kind
A very rare treat

But I had to realize
He wasn't deserving
And for the rest of his life
He would continue searching

But never truly finding
Close, but not quite
A woman like me
That could've been his wife

The next chick that came along
I encouraged him to propose

The Dual Sides of My Gemini Mind

Dating that girl thirteen years
She was happy, I suppose

He invited me to the wedding
Wanted me to be a guest
Never would I ever
Stayed away, for the best

We made better friends
Than we ever were lovers
It took a while, but
We finally got over each other

First loves can be hard to shake
He was my first love
As well as
My very first heartbreak

LaRhonda N. Felton

The Dual Sides of My Gemini Mind

Mind Made Up

My life is out of sorts
Almost like driving blind
Imagine driving without an alignment
And a very cloudy mind

Going here and there
Without laying roots
No distinct definition
My path misconstrued

As I sit and ponder
On this grand catastrophe
I stumble upon this video
And suddenly I have an epiphany

I need to make decisions
And I need to have a plan
A map to chart my way
Take my destiny into my hands

Don't leave decisions to others
And I won't stop and wait

LaRhonda N. Felton

Do what I need to today
For tomorrow may be too late

Throw caution to the wind
And be prepared for success
I can never consider it a loss
When I'm doing my very best
Because when I don't at least try
The answer is always no
By putting myself out there
Who knows how far I could go?

From now on, moving forward
I will chart my way
Since things could change day to day

But having this outline
Will truly help me see
There are bigger and better things
Waiting in store for me

So, if you, too, feel scattered
Like you've lost your way
Become the captain of your life

The Dual Sides of My Gemini Mind

Don't put it off another day

Some people have wasted a lifetime
On what could've been
To suddenly wake up
And only have, *I remember when*

I don't want that for my life
So I decided to make this change
I'm saving myself
And I'm starting today

LaRhonda N. Felton

The Dual Sides of My Gemini Mind

Bedroom Shenanigans

He is deep inside of me
And I'm delirious with passion
He knows exactly what I need
He's putting it down in proper fashion

I push him deeper with my hands on his ass
It's almost more than I can bear
He moans out loud
While he grips my hair

Our love making is intense
We're both so turned on
He feels amazing
I can't help but moan

He knows what's coming
And he speeds up the pace
Right when I climax
He pulls out to use his face

It was like before I could move

LaRhonda N. Felton

His tongue was in my pussy
I came so hard
Even his beard was gushy

He turns me over
Our absolute favorite: prone bone
Smacking my ass hard
Fucking me from behind and making me moan
He asks me how it feels
It's like I'm on top of the world
I'm cumming again
He makes my toes curl

"Baby, it's so good," I say
As I beg him to fuck me
He does just that
Like he hates to love me

He says your pussy is swelling
And he knows I'm about to cum
He smacks my ass hard
As I come undone

The Dual Sides of My Gemini Mind

I squeeze my pussy tight
I know he can't hold on
I feel him cum inside me
Releasing all his little ones

He falls beside me
Kisses my lips
We are each other's freaks
And we love this shit

LaRhonda N. Felton

The Dual Sides of My Gemini Mind

Pendulum

He won't commit
But he won't let you go
What is it you're doing?
What are you hanging on for?

You pull away
And he sucks you back in
Dangling just enough
Keeping you guessin'

Does he want to be your man?
Or is he running game
Does he want you as his woman?
The back and forth is so lame

You question him
On what it is he wants
He has all the right answers
Or is it all just a front

To see how far he can get
How far you allow it to go

LaRhonda N. Felton

Before you crack under pressure
When you can't stand anymore

The constant back and forth
Has you mixed up and confused
What's the title for this
Indecisive abuse?
A man that won't commit
That won't just step into the light
Watching you struggle with the what ifs
Is he even worth the fight?

Maybe you should choose
Simply end your misery
Stop the swing of the pendulum
And make his ass history

Forewarned

He sent me a warning
And I should've taken heed
It literally said
You might fall in love with me

I read it when he sent it
At the time I actually laughed
I had no clue
Falling in love was in my path

OK, I knew I liked him
Quite a lot, I will admit
But my heart betrayed me
I fell very deep and much too quick

I know I can't place a timeline
On how fast love can appear
He makes me happy
But I am full of fear

This is a totally different space
I've never had a connection this deep

LaRhonda N. Felton

I've heard that they existed
Just never thought it would be me

It feels like I've known him
From another place and time
And from the minute I laid eyes on him
I knew he was mine
I didn't know how it would happen
Or when it would unfold
There's something very deep between us
If truth should be told

So, if I had known all of this
Why am I afraid?
Because love has eluded me
For so many decades

I've been in love before
But never quite like this
He knows things no one else does
A fact I can't dismiss

So, that warning he sent to me
Has become absolute truth

The Dual Sides of My Gemini Mind

I have fallen in love with him
I only pray he feels the same way too

LaRhonda N. Felton

Purple

I woke up thinking of him
My heart bursting at the seams
I love him so much
With every fiber of my being

I'm not sure if he will remain mine
Or even how long this will last
I'm enjoying what we have now
I can't dwell on what may come to pass

I write about love all the time
Yet, describing this I can't find the words
And for me that seems
Honestly speaking, downright absurd

He inspires me like no other
Takes my breath away
He puts a smile on my face
From the moment that I wake

I'm afraid of what this means
Or how I go on if it ends

LaRhonda N. Felton

But I can't focus on the what ifs
I must rely on what is

The fact of the matter
He is my purple, my absolute favorite
I see him in everything
This feeling is the greatest
Loving him has me both
Afraid and so excited
The fact that it is love
Deny it? I wouldn't dare try it

We were connected from the beginning
Like our souls had met their match
I somehow knew he belonged to me
God whispered that fact

He let me know, it wouldn't be easy
But that I shouldn't give up
He is what I needed
A blessing, nothing to do with luck

But no single love story is perfect
There will be ebbs and flows

The Dual Sides of My Gemini Mind

There will be tough days ahead
How we survive them? Only God knows

But if we're willing to work through
By sacrificing and dedicating the time
I will remain his
And he will remain mine
My purple is the only one
That sets my soul on fire
Days filled with love
Nights full of passion and desire

I know we all have a favorite
If not, then you need to
Maybe yours is iridescent
Or a beautiful azure blue

Whatever color you land on
My hope is that it will last
I'm going now to snuggle with purple
He's one handsome, sexy lad

Who Is He?

I'm fighting myself not to love him
But he's so damn charming
Bad for me at the same time
My defenses, he's disarming

I can't allow him to leave me
Just swinging in the wind
I won't play the fool this time
Not even for him

What makes him so special?
What is it I can't ignore?
What is the purpose of this?
What did he come into my life for?

Was it to teach me a lesson
Push me past my fears
Make me fall in love
And leave me in tears?

I have cut myself off
So many times in the past

LaRhonda N. Felton

I don't know if I can do it again
I thought this time would be the last

The last time for me
Playing silly love games
I thought this one could end
With me taking his last name
Here I am again
Seemingly playing the fool
He's so nonchalant and cold
Playing it real cool

It takes everything in me
Not to reach out and check in
But I must maintain my pride
Can't feel like I'm beggin'

I'm putting me first
I must stick to that plan
Can't let my life become
Obsessed with loving this man

In His Arms

I'm on 95, the weather's turned mean
It's raining so hard, I can't see a thing
A vibrating phone interrupts my thoughts
He says, "I knew if you left in the storm, you'd be caught
Come back baby, it's dangerous out
I need you here, not out and about"

I say, "The next exit isn't for miles"
As I listen to his voice all I can do is smile
He won't hang up, refusing to lose the connection
All I wanted was his love and affection
His voice is calming, and I feel safe
Being in his arms is my favorite place

He's telling me to pull over, he'll come for me
I say, "Baby it's a mess out, traffic is maddening"
"Put me on Bluetooth, but don't hang up"
He commands me as traffic ahead stops abrupt
I don't tell him what happened, fearing he'd lose it
I stay focused on his voice, for me it's so soothing

LaRhonda N. Felton

I just want to be in his arms and that's all
He asks if I'm OK, I say, "Yes", that's best
If I say much more, he will hear my stress
I see my exit approaching
And this rain is pouring

He asks, "Baby can you hear me?"
Shaking my thoughts from my reverie
"Yes, baby, I hear you, I'll be back there soon"
Not soon enough, these clouds look like doom
Slowly but surely, it's a creep and a crawl
"How much further?" he asks
"Take the back roads on your way back"

Suddenly there's lightning, and our connection is gone
I needed his voice to keep me calm
I try calling back to no avail
As luck would have it, the rain turns to hail
I follow his instructions and take the back roads
A semi on its side has lost its load
My phone rings once, and the call drops
I would do anything for this storm to stop

The Dual Sides of My Gemini Mind

About seven more minutes, and I'll be there
Safely in his arms, without a worry or a care
I ask myself, *when did I fall in love?*
I don't remember
April, May, August or December?
Either way I'm here, and I can't turn around
I love everything about him, from his smile to his frown

Thoughts of him to pass the time
A few more minutes and I'll be just fine
I see the sign indicating my destination
I turn left without hesitation
He's standing in the driveway, freezing in the storm
I will cuddle him close to get him warm
Soaking wet, he opens my car door
I fall into his arms, longing no more

The Dual Sides of My Gemini Mind

Ain't It Funny

What is it about the ones you upgrade?
Always scheming, cheating and throwing shade
Could it be I gave him too much credit?
And never once did I sweat it
That you weren't there for me

Could it be that once I realized?
The disguise and all the lies
I got the hell up the road
No longer your girl
I have a brand-new world
Love in excess and overload

So, you can surely kick rocks
In open-toed flip flops
And watch me from afar
Don't come too close
Stalk my page and watch me post
Happy life events that don't include you
Continue living my life is what I will do
I won't wallow in self pity

LaRhonda N. Felton

Why should I? Hell, I'm too pretty
To allow one parasite to end my parade
Especially one I had to come in and upgrade

Sex Scene Part II

And the scene continues
He's still on top
Slow, long strokes
His tongue in my mouth
Suddenly with a shift
He switches our position
He wants me bent over
Hitting me from the back has him on a mission

Long, deep strokes
Making me call his name
He quickens his pace
I cum yet again
I'm rubbing my clit
He's in a zone
He calls my name
Sex got his mind gone

I push my ass back
To meet his thrusts
Squeezing those inner muscles
Music playing, we're lost in lust

LaRhonda N. Felton

He's slapping my ass
Making me scream his name
I bury my face in the pillows
While I cum once again

The sounds are outrageous
I feel like I'm peeing
After this marathon
Will be some damn good sleeping

But before we get there
I must even the score
Make him cum hard
Pelvic muscles squeezing him more

I hear the change in his breathing
He's tapping out soon
He is gripping my hips
Our sex music fills the room
In and out of my body, he goes
The nut that's approaching
Is coming up from his toes

"Oh shit," he yells

The Dual Sides of My Gemini Mind

His pace hard and fast
I feel him tremble inside me as he pulls out
And spreads the warmth all over my ass

LaRhonda N. Felton

The Dual Sides of My Gemini Mind

Unplugged

I plugged into an outlet
That had a power surge
It zapped every ounce of my energy
And severely frayed my nerves
I didn't turn away
Although I knew I should
But even with the pain and darkness
Parts of it felt so good
I remained plugged in
To a source that burned
The connection was tight
It seems I hadn't learned
How to recharge myself
Without it being toxic
No matter what I told myself
Somehow, I couldn't stop it

My alarm didn't ring
Due to misuse of power
I missed important messages
They went unread for hours
I needed to find a retreat

LaRhonda N. Felton

A way to disconnect
Before I lost everything
Including my self-respect
That's when I smelled the burning
And I felt a very hard shove
I'm coming to my senses
My love has finally unplugged

Awakened

Something has me stirring
That dream was getting good
What could it be?
I was alone when I fell asleep

It's cold and it's wet
I need to open my eyes
Needless, to say my boo is wild
He's rubbing ice between my thighs

He notices I'm now awake
"Shhh," he says
I'm quiet
I can see he wants to play

He's so cute
And sexy as hell
I'm quiet for him
But I want to yell

LaRhonda N. Felton

He's in charge
I will be patient, wait and see
Exactly what he has in store for me
Good ol' lovin'
It seems he's been craving
And myself, only for him
I've been saving

He was in my dream
Which is why I didn't want to wake
But reality over fantasy
I'll choose real any day

Imagine my surprise
To find him in my room
Making sweet love to me
In the middle of the afternoon

The Dual Sides of My Gemini Mind

Emotionally Unavailable

I sit back and observe
Waiting for his next move
Watching and listening
To see what he's willing to do

Will he fight for me?
Will he fight for us?
Or turn back and run
Deciding we're not worth the fuss

I don't need him if he's afraid
Too scared to be hurt
I need him to be ready to go to battle
With all of those that will test our worth

Show and prove that we're strong
Harder than marble or granite
Show them all we won't be broken
Haters are watching, and they can't stand the sight

LaRhonda N. Felton

I need to know he thinks I'm worthy
To be his only one
To fight our nightmares under the moon
Waking under the rays of a beautiful sun

I don't have my answers just yet
We have countless similarities, and are very relatable
Although the question constantly lingers
Is he emotionally unavailable?

The Dual Sides of My Gemini Mind

Side Pieces

No girl wants to be alone
But all these boys want is to bone
Sex you up, leaving you high and dry
Just ghost, not even a proper goodbye

It all begins with that *WYD* text
That leads to a late night of meaningless sex
You're trying to build
He had time to kill
He never takes you out
That's not what this is about

You've made it too easy, became a receptacle
For his emoji that's described using a vegetable
But you don't qualify for a corner seat at his table
He calls you off the bench
When the first string is unavailable

Late at night once its pitch-black dark
You're killing yourself, auditioning for this small part
Thinking you can sex your way into first place
Meanwhile, the main chick is flaunted in your face

LaRhonda N. Felton

He knows if you don't, someone else will
You wonder what she has that makes him pay her bills
You lay back and simply wait
Praying she makes that unforgivable mistake
Sad thing is, you got this shit so twisted
You're just a number on his list of numerous side bitches

Don't think it's a secret, his wife knew all along
She gets hers in too, allowing that dog to roam
When shit hits the fan, she's cool, calm and ready to collect
After all, she's the payee on the alimony check

So, while you sell yourself short being the side chick
Thinking you're winning,
While being loyal to community dick
He's on to the next, preparing to buy her a house
You learn she's next in line for the title of spouse
Where do you fit in all of this you ask?
Baby wake up, you were merely a piece of ass

The Dual Sides of My Gemini Mind

Long Distance

I lie in the bed alone
Wishing you were here
Suddenly my vision blurs
And my cheeks are covered in tears

I miss you so much
Needing to breathe in your scent
Clean, cool and crisp
Like the center of a peppermint

What can I do?
When every waking moment
Is consumed with thoughts of you
I go to bed alone
In my dreams, you're there too

I feel lonely and weak
What has caused this wicked addiction?
Falling in love with you
Has finally come to fruition
But it's causing me heartbreak

LaRhonda N. Felton

Bringing me pain
When I long to touch you
I reach out in vain

This situation isn't for everyone
It takes patience and dedication
If I could be with you every night
I would without hesitation
We must be creative
And constantly persistent
Because we're in a relationship
That requires long distance

The Dual Sides of My Gemini Mind

He Is Home

When I can't hear his voice
I read what he's written
Suffice it to say I'm in love
So far past smitten

When I can't see his face
I stare at his pics in my phone
Waiting for the day we share the same address
The place we call home

When I can't sleep without him
It's of him I dream
God knows it's him I need
So, he brings us together in each scene

When I'm having a bad day
And he sends a random text
Allowing me to vent my issues
Some days I'm so vexed

When I lie in bed
Talking to God

LaRhonda N. Felton

I'm praying for him
Some days can be very hard
When I'm not expecting it
He lets me know
It won't be much longer
He's getting on the road

When I'm in his arms
No other place I'd rather be
I know I belong there
Because he is home to me

The Dual Sides of My Gemini Mind

Too Late

This is something I must get out
Or I will die in silence
I really want to do him bodily harm
But I'm not prone to violence

Anger so deep, it's digging at my soul
Trying to consume me
But I will leave it all on paper
In the lines of my poetry

Boy meets girl
And all that other good shit
Thought I was done being played
But this negro wasn't having it

Wrapped himself perfectly
Appeared as everything I needed
And once again, silly me
Left my heart open to take the beating

Oh, he was suave with his approach
And on the outside, so damn fine

LaRhonda N. Felton

But I should've looked a bit deeper
I mean really took my time

He is damaged goods
Right from the very start
If I knew then what I know now
I would've never played a part

He gave me some clues
So, I accept some of the blame
And if I'm completely honest
I should've stayed in my lane

From his very first lie
I should've deleted his name
But his lying ass is very good
At his woe is me game

The consummate victim
Hurting from his past
I should've called him on his shit
But I was in love, down for his ass

The Dual Sides of My Gemini Mind

More down than I've ever been
For any man in my life
He got me this time
I'll be damned if he gets me twice

I'm all cried out
I'm writing this one with dry eyes
Because I gave it all I had
I won't waste any more time

Listening to his lame ass excuses
Reading his bullshit via text
I am doing what needs to be done
And moving on to the next

It's crystal clear to me
I am not the woman he wants
And it hurts like hell
I can't even front

The loving was damn good
The best I've ever had
But that isn't enough for me
With his disrespectful ass

LaRhonda N. Felton

He said we had something special
And I believed him like a fool
His actions say otherwise
Hell, what would you do?

I must cut my losses
And heal my heartache
When he tries to come back
I'm saying, "Negro please, it's too late"

The Dual Sides of My Gemini Mind

Bad Idea

I'm lying on my back
Thinking, *what is he doing*?
My clit isn't a ribeye
Do I hear chewing?

He's looking up at my face
For a sign of satisfaction
I tap him on his shoulder
To quickly kill this action

If he's this bad at head
It hurts to imagine the rest
And I'm no crash dummy
I didn't sign up for this test

I gather up my clothes
And he's lying there looking clueless
He asks, "Are you leaving?"
I started to say, "Yeah stupid"

But I didn't want to hurt his feelings
He's wasted enough of my time

LaRhonda N. Felton

It's my own fault
I should've followed my first mind

I said, "Yes, I need to leave"
This was a very bad idea
I thought I was ready for this
But I'm not over him
And in my head
Was an entirely different thought
Sex with you will be wack as hell
And I refuse to suffer the loss

He paid for the hotel
And that's money he's wasted
Because Champagne required expert attention
And he wasn't qualified to taste it

Lapping and chewing
Like my clit was a stick of gum
He didn't possess the finesse
To possibly make me cum
It seems karma played a part
Or either I played myself
I had a soul snatcher waiting

The Dual Sides of My Gemini Mind

And I'm testing out someone else
Soul snatcher had caller earlier
Asking about my plans for the evening
I told him I was heading out
He didn't need to know who I was seeing

I got in my car
Thankful that I drove myself
The nibbler can try that on another chick
Or someone else
Once inside my car
I gave soul snatcher a ring
He answered like he always does
Hey baby what's happening

I said my plans fell through
Asked if he wanted to come by
Said I would be home in a few
I needed to see him, that was no lie
I showered and dressed
In something I knew he would like
Because once he arrived

LaRhonda N. Felton

It would be an amazing night
The nibbler was blocked
And I bid him adieu
As I dialed my sister crying laughing
She answered what did you do?
I told her about the nibbler
And that soul snatcher was on his way here
We laughed until my doorbell rang
At my initial bad idea

The Dual Sides of My Gemini Mind

Needing More

As he's walking out the door
My heart is breaking
I want to yell, "Stop"
I can't stop shaking

I love him so much
Our time together is short
I want him all the time
A few hours are our last resort

He came in for a day
I took off from work
The moment he entered the door
We both went berserk

A quick hello
A smile exchanged
I pushed him against the wall
Very wild and untamed

We used our time wisely
Not wasting a minute

LaRhonda N. Felton

As usual, it was over too soon
And our time together had ended
We made our way to the door
To say our goodbyes
I looked away from him
To keep from crying
He kissed my lips
Until next time
I watched him leave
It blew my mind

I came back in
Cleaned up traces where we made love
Startling me from the process
My phone started to buzz

It was a text from him
A smile came over my face
We discussed the events of the entire day
And scheduled a meeting for the next time and place

The Dual Sides of My Gemini Mind

Love All Over

I don't want a relationship like everyone else's
I want it to be desired
For us to be the example
Of love and passionate fire

I don't want perfection
Because that doesn't exist
But when you think of the love of your life
My name needs to be first on that list

I want a mutual understanding
For what we both stand to lose
I want when push comes to shove
It's me that you choose

Fight for us
Let it be known I'm your girl
You're my man
And I will shout that to the world

Yet, I feel alone
Like your best kept secret

LaRhonda N. Felton

You couldn't care less
As if my presence is not needed

Show me how bad you want me
Forever, as yours to keep
Love seen all over us
From our heads down to our feet
I love having you in my life
I just need to know you feel the same
And to know a smile crosses your face
At the mere mention of my name

The Dual Sides of My Gemini Mind

Brokenhearted

I lie in bed alone
As tears soak my face
I don't understand why this keeps happening
Me back in the same place

Alone and confused
Not knowing why
With all the failed relationships
And your need to lie

What is it about me?
That you can leave so carefree
No word, no explanation
It's so disheartening

I have put on a brave front
For far too many days
And I haven't heard from him
Not even a simple "Hey"

My heart is bursting
And I feel so sad

LaRhonda N. Felton

Why did he do this to me?
Is being with me that bad?

Rhetorical question
Because I know I'm a great catch
I just can't figure out
Why this lesson keeps coming back
Maybe I should argue more
Act like a crazy bitch
But that's not who I am
This is some bullshit

Maybe this is his out
How he wanted it to end
Maybe it shouldn't have started
And I wouldn't be left wonderin'

What did I do?
And where did I go wrong?
I wouldn't be lying here at 3AM
Singing this same sad ass song

I'm so sick of this shit
Him winning and me zero

The Dual Sides of My Gemini Mind

I want to be in love and happy
Where is my fairytale hero?

Maybe when I'm too old
And I give zero fucks
But here I am broken hearted
And this really sucks

He's living his life
And I'm saving myself
What the hell for?
Because I can't see myself loving anyone else

This is it though
Fuck love and being faithful
I'm ready for the next man
That's ready, willing, and able

This time has changed me
In some ways for the worse
Because from here on out
I'm putting me first

First before his feelings

LaRhonda N. Felton

First before his needs
You can thank the liars from my past
Change my mind? Bitch please!

You have used and depleted me
My love well is dry
As my heart continues to break
All I can do is cry

I hate him for this
And I hate me a little more
I wish I didn't care at all
I am broken to my core

I trusted him implicitly
And he broke my heart
I feel disintegrated, shattered
Completely ripped apart

My pillow is soaked
My face is a mess
My eyes are swollen
And I feel depressed

The Dual Sides of My Gemini Mind

But I can't stop writing
I don't know why
Maybe because it hurts so much
To have to say goodbye

I was good for a while
I thought the tears were done
Then thoughts return of him
And the sobs just come

He has hurt me badly
And he doesn't even know
He probably doesn't care
And that fact hurts even more

I can't talk to anyone
I feel so stupid
And to think of what I've done for him
I feel downright foolish

God, please help me
Please ease this pain
I don't EVER want to feel
This broken again

LaRhonda N. Felton

I'm begging you, Father
This is more than I can bear

Erase my memories
Of him ever being there

Wipe the slate clean
He didn't deserve me
And I don't deserve this pain
At the level I'm hurting

My heart is racing
And I can't breathe
Stop the tears
So I can sleep, please!

A few deep breaths
And my heart slows its pace
The tears continue their descent
Down the middle of my face
I hate that I love him
And that is my absolute truth
I wish that I could hate him
Because once again, I feel like a fool

The Dual Sides of My Gemini Mind

Levels

I need attention
And reassurance
I need a strong man
With some endurance

He can't be afraid of love
And he can't be afraid to prove
He needs to love all of me
Not just the parts he approves

I'm multi-faceted
I have a lot of layers
He needs to be able to handle me
And my many assorted flavors

Some days I'm confident
Other days, not so much
He needs to know what I need
With the exact right touch

That most days
I want him to lead

LaRhonda N. Felton

Other days I need him
To just listen to me

Not provide a solution
But just let me vent
Make time for us
Time that's well spent
So, I need love
In many ways
The level of that love
Well, it depends on the day

The Dual Sides of My Gemini Mind

Privileges Revoked

We're laughing and talking
The vibe is very deep
I find myself thinking of you
Even in my sleep

We progress and move forward
To the point of making love
Even that feels like a fantasy
But that won't be enough

I hold you down
I mean really have your back
Showing that I'm in your corner
Proving what I say to be fact

Do you appreciate it?
No, not really
You bitch up quick
Are you that cold and unfeeling?

I'm learning a lot
Especially that I don't have the tools

LaRhonda N. Felton

I don't know how to love you
And I refuse to look like a fool

You open a little
And shut tight like a clam
No matter how much I care
It's like you don't give a damn
So, maybe I'm not her
The woman for you
Maybe you're too jaded
And you don't know exactly what to do

The benefit of the doubt
Has been given and revoked
I can't keep giving you my love
And holding on to hope

One of these days
I won't be waiting in the wings
Sooner, rather than later
You will surely miss me

It's happened before
And it will happen again

The Dual Sides of My Gemini Mind

You will reach back out
Supposedly checking on a *friend*

Asking what I'm up to
Wondering if I have a man
And what caused us to be over
Will be so hard for you to understand

As if I didn't give you enough time
To get your shit together
I will laugh it off
Like, "Yeah whatever"

Because you've had time
To keep me in your world
So, miss me with the bullshit
Obviously, I wasn't the right girl

LaRhonda N. Felton

Deeper

He's kissing me deeply
His hand up my skirt
I cum so hard
I rip three buttons off his shirt
His tongue is in my mouth
Ooh, it's so hot
I'm convulsing so hard
And I can't stop

He keeps stroking me
Deeper and deeper
My body is on fire
Like a winter night's heater
I moan and squirm
Trying to get away
He grips my ass
And he whispers, "Stay"

My body can't take much more
What does he want?
He looks deep into my eyes
And continues to taunt

LaRhonda N. Felton

The climax is building
My body wants this
He feels the flood
And deepens his kiss
He flips me over
And with a quick move
He's deep inside matching my groove
His rhythm is on point
I can't hold back
I'm suddenly hit
With a body-shattering climax

He's not yet done
But I'm almost tapped
He increases his speed
Gives my ass a slap

He grips my hips
And drives deeper inside
My eyes close in ecstasy
It feels so good I could cry

He reaches around
And strokes me more

The Dual Sides of My Gemini Mind

I shudder so hard
We almost hit the floor

My heart is racing
His pace is fast
He moans and curses
Once again, slapping my ass

We fall in a heap
Still half undressed
The sandman arrives
We need the rest

The Dual Sides of My Gemini Mind

Follow My Heart

I stand here, while he's gazing in my eyes
Knowing I can't take these vows
To spend the rest of my life
I love him, but not enough to stay
Not enough to wake up to every single day

I should've said no, when he proposed
It was the magic of the moment, I suppose

Him down on bended knee
In front of our entire families
What did I expect?
Now, I'm filled with nothing but regret

I'm standing here looking for an out
Being his wife is not what my life is about
Then I see him coming down the aisle
He's looking at me with a half frown, half smile

What the hell is he thinking?
My heart is happy, but my fear is increasing
He steps in, looks me in my eyes

LaRhonda N. Felton

Asking me, "Baby what are you doing with this guy?"

My fiancée grips my hands
He's looking at me, like *who is this man*?
We can't do this here, I need to leave
But my feet won't move, and I can't breathe

I wish I could disappear, I can feel all eyes on me
But it's not my fiancée that I want to marry
I say, "I can't", and begin to walk away
My fiancée yells, "Is this what you meant the other day?"

Why didn't I tell him? I can't look back
I'm getting daggers from his family, that's a fact
A hand on my back rushes me along
I hear my best friend start to sing a song

I must follow my heart
Which I should've done from the start
From now on I will take heed and not falter
Remembering the day, I ran from the altar

Us

He is broken
And so am I
Some nights I lay in bed
And tears fill my eyes
I want to fix him
But I don't have the tools
Too many dark areas
And so many rules

He wants to fix me
But he doesn't have all the pieces
Too many words unsaid
For a myriad of reasons
So, we silently acquiesce
In our individual gloom
As we both lie in bed
Alone in our room

We smile and laugh
Putting the best outside
We're both screaming inside
Complete happiness denied

LaRhonda N. Felton

Where do we start?

To come out of the illusion
To repair the damage
And reach a conclusion
To appreciate our brokenness
Accepting of our flaws
Finally allowing true healing
Of our emotional scars

I want to fix him
He wants to fix me
It's like solving a puzzle
We begin with the first piece

The Dual Sides of My Gemini Mind

Soulmate

We met as strangers
In an unfamiliar place
Yet, our hearts begin to beat
At a strange but symmetrical pace

How was this possible?
We knew nothing about each other
Yet our hearts did this dance
Like remembering a former lover

With intensity so strong
It was somewhat frightening
Becoming a magnetic attraction
Fused together by lightning

I didn't know him
And he didn't know me
So strange, yet so familiar
Burning like electricity

We couldn't stop talking
We had so much to say

LaRhonda N. Felton

Life stories and laughter
We couldn't do it all in one day

He pursued conversation
I think we knew all along
Since this attraction was too strong
To let bygones be bygones
I'm glad he took the chance
And reached out to me
Allowing us to explore
Exactly where this could lead

We didn't ignore the obvious
And we couldn't suppress the attraction
We're doing the right thing
By putting the thought into action

The Dual Sides of My Gemini Mind

Second Thoughts

We both know it was over
We just wouldn't admit it
Who would keep the house?
We sure as hell couldn't split it

Assets and break ups
Some would rather hide than divide
We still loved each other
A fact that neither of us denied

Somewhere along the way
We both got lost
And now our life together
Is paying the cost

Handling things on the surface
Refusing to dig deep
Promising ourselves a better tomorrow
Before we fall asleep

Be we never faced the issues
We put off until another day

LaRhonda N. Felton

Now we don't know where to begin
Or even what to say

My lawyer contacted his
After we said we were done
We haven't had one conversation
Not a single, solitary one
Irreconcilable differences
The reason used for our divorce
We just went about our day
Letting the events take their course

So, we sit at this table
Him with his team and me with mine
Looking over documents
Just watching the time

He looks at me
And I turn away
Wanting to erase
The events of this day

He asks for a moment
For us to be alone

The Dual Sides of My Gemini Mind

He says to me
"Baby let's just go home"

I look at him
And ask, "What are you saying?"
He repeats, "I want us to go home
And I'm not playing
What are we doing here?
This isn't who we are
We've been together too long
And we've come too far."

I look at him and ask
"Do you think we stand a chance?"
He says, "With you by my side
You bet your sweet ass
I love you
And you love me
Let's go back in there
And cancel this thing."

So, that's just what we did
Came to our senses
Canceled the divorce

LaRhonda N. Felton

And laughed off the expenses

That night, we had a carpet picnic
On our bedroom floor
We reminisced about
The love that we adore

The Dual Sides of My Gemini Mind

His & Hers

He makes me think of making love
And very passionate sex
We're constantly turning each other on
Through videos and text
And when we get together
We are on a mission
Hugging, touching and lots of kissing

He takes off our clothes
We're both dying to get him inside
He makes sure I'm gushy
With his face between my thighs
He slides in
My breath in my throat
I feel every inch
As he begins a slow stroke

I whisper, "Right there, baby
Please, don't stop"
He knows just what to do
And he keeps hitting my spot

LaRhonda N. Felton

I moan his name
As I close my eyes
He has me in a trance
I'm almost hypnotized

Right now, I belong to him
He is my master
And my body feels the pleasure
As his pace becomes faster
He moans my name
As he kisses me deeply
This feels so amazing
I'm his completely

Our bodies are in tune
With the same thing in mind
And that's reaching our climax
At the exact same time
I don't make him pull out
He can cum inside
Because I belong to him
And he is most assuredly mine

His Breaking Point

We're making love
And something changed
Suddenly I felt all his hurt
And all his pain
Pushing deep inside
He's now trusting me
Letting me in
Revealing his history

His body starts to heave
He begins to shake and cry
I don't even question it
I know the reasons why
The pain he's endured
From a boy to a man
I hold him tighter
He knows I understand

My shoulder is wet
From him shedding tears
Letting go of the past
Hurt throughout the years

LaRhonda N. Felton

He holds me tighter
His cries turn to sobs
As he mourns the little boy
Whose life was robbed

Forced to be a man
Long before his time
He can be vulnerable with me
He knows I don't mind

My tears fill my ears
I can't erase his pain
He needs this release
To feel whole again

I lie underneath him
It's OK, I can wait
Until he feels he can speak
I share his heartbreak

It's like everything he feels
Passes through me
I don't hold it in
I catch and release

The Dual Sides of My Gemini Mind

He looks into my eyes
And quickly looks away
He doesn't know how to feel
Or even what to say

I reassure him
As I kiss his tears
"I'm proud of you baby
For releasing your fears"

I hold him close
He finally feels at peace
I rock him gently
Until he falls asleep

The Dual Sides of My Gemini Mind

Untrustworthy

I love him
And he lied
It broke my heart
Confused my pride

If you haven't experienced it
You simply can't understand
The pain a woman feels
When she's been hurt by her man

The one I've loved
I gave him my all
This pain slices my heart
My trust has taken a fall

I don't know myself
My anger I'm trying to contain
At least for the moment
But I'm in so much pain

He keeps apologizing
It doesn't really help

LaRhonda N. Felton

Because he has no idea
Of the amount of pain he's dealt

He won't go far
Even when I ask for space
He keeps hanging around
A constant reminder in my face
The pain of lies
Sometimes never heal
But you had to have been there
To understand how I feel

The Dual Sides of My Gemini Mind

Quiet as Kept

It happened one night
We met at a party
We were with other people
Is how the whole thing started

He was with someone
And so was I
Yet we kept sneaking looks
Giving each other the eye

Somehow, we managed
To sneak away time
I refused to take his number
Instead, giving him mine

We met up, he questioned my life
I, in turn, asked about his
He has two sons
I don't have any kids

These random meetings
Kept taking place

LaRhonda N. Felton

We would meet after work
Or for coffee and lunch dates

We both knew
We were getting in too deep
But the attraction was wicked
We just had to meet

So, I got a second phone
To cut down confusion
He got another phone, too
Just to keep up the illusion

We were both unhappy
In our current situation
So we made plans
To meet up on vacation

He convinced his wife
I convinced my man
This year's destination
Would be one in sun and sand

The Dual Sides of My Gemini Mind

We each rented a cabin
A block away from each other
We couldn't risk being caught
By our significant lovers

There was a hotel
Not too far away
We would sneak in a visit
Just about every day

One afternoon
We almost got caught
His wife was buying flowers
From the hotel flower shop

Day number three
My man was on my case
Claiming we're on vacation
Yet, I'm all over the place

We met up on the last night
And decided the deceit needed to stop
We talked, and we cried
We kissed each other a lot

LaRhonda N. Felton

I get back to my cabin
Planning to make an excuse
Yet, I'm stepping over clothes
And a pair of very cute shoes

The outdoor shower is going
I'm thinking, in the middle of the night?
I look into my husband's eyes
And the eyes of my ex-lover's wife

The Dual Sides of My Gemini Mind

Killing the Vibe

Let me explain something
I want your love, but I won't beg
I will merely walk away
And in my mind, you're dead
No longer breathing
You cease to exist
No birthdays to remember
Deleted from my list

I won't tell you why
You should already know
I explained my expectations
From the get-go
So, don't blame me
For throwing the relationship in the ditch
You are beating me mad
And somehow, I'm the bitch?

Stop playing the victim
Own your truth lil' baby
Because all along
You were being shady

LaRhonda N. Felton

My love for you wasn't a secret
A fact you can't deny
You slipped and dismissed it
And now you are wondering why

I don't call or check in
Or trip like I used to
When I'm done it's a wrap
I tried to tell you, boo boo

Now all you need to do
Is face your newly single life
I may play the fool once
But I'll be damned if it's twice

The Dual Sides of My Gemini Mind

Your Worst Nightmare

I'll be her
Savage and don't give a fuck
No longer protecting your feelings
You're shit out of luck

I'll be her
The bitch you grow to hate
Don't act surprised
Hey, you made me this way

I'll be her
Not giving in to you
Didn't think I had it in me?
Shit, you don't have a clue

I'll be her
The bitch you don't recognize
I hate you hate it
It's me you now despise

I'll be her
Partying with your friends

LaRhonda N. Felton

You don't know me
And they become a means to an end

I'll be her
The nightmare keeping you awake
You started this shit
I'm ending it my way
I'll be her
Making you wish I was dead
Cause I'm your neurologist
A PHD to get inside your head

I'll be her
Always two steps away
And then right behind you
Just when you thought it was safe

Don't make me become her
And all will be well
Otherwise, your quiet life
Will become a living hell

The Dual Sides of My Gemini Mind

Historically Speaking

Can you ever love unconditionally
When you haven't gotten over your past?
Will you ever put someone before you
Or will everyone else continue to come last?

You are a complete and total mess
Yet, you expect to be accepted
But in others you want perfection
Or they will face your insolent rejection

Do you realize just how shallow you are?
Only loving on the surface
You're too afraid to dig deeper
The fact is, hell, we're all imperfect

We all have shit to sort through
Such as pain and unwanted baggage
I was willing to accept it all
I was also willing to help you carry it

But I became your empath
The one you came to and dumped

LaRhonda N. Felton

All your bad days, weeks and months
I really feel like a chump

I loved you and I listened
Tried to be your backbone
Not realizing that you had other plans
I was a mere stepping stone

You used and abused my love
You assumed you'd never lose it
And I played my part in it
Thinking we would work through it

I refused to listen to my own intuition
And gave you so many excuses
Knowing how much I loved you
I didn't want to see what your truth is

That you're selfish and you aren't ready
Fact is, maybe you never will be
To give the type of love that I need
The loving adoration of which I'm so worthy

The Dual Sides of My Gemini Mind

This truth comes from my heart
And it's a hurtful realization at last
That you won't ever experience real love
Until you find the courage to deal with your past

On the Edge

I'm feeling tired
And completely worn out
I keep pushing
Day in and day out
When can I rest?
Clear my mind
Everything taking up
Too much of my me time

I need peace
Yes, peace and quiet
My brain is full of noise
A constant fucking riot
Who looks after me?
Who makes sure I'm OK?
Like a stereo with no stop button
I'm constantly on play

When can I get off?
Throw it all in and quit
Let someone else think a while
I'm tired of all this shit

LaRhonda N. Felton

The job and the bills
Always on the go
I need a break from it all
My body's telling me so

I lay in bed
With plans to go to sleep
Closing my eyes
And the thoughts begin to creep

Did you do this?
Did you do that?
It never shuts off
My nerves are racked
I need a moment
Some quiet alone time
Before the pressures of it all
Make me lose my damn mind

The Dual Sides of My Gemini Mind

Indica

Induced haze
Embracing the day
Watching the palm trees sway
He loves when I'm this way

Eyes so low, almost closed
Shotgun ganja to the nose
Everything around me slows
As he removes my clothes

His hands on my skin
I puff and pass to him again
He chokes, and I grin
He inhaled too hard just then

We smoke, and we play
The grown and sexy way
No interruptions today
Just me and my baby

Sipping and smoking
Kissing and stroking

LaRhonda N. Felton

Between my legs, a sensual explosion

As we drift off tangled and tired
Fulfilling each other's desires
The air filled with Indica fire
Not for everyone, the taste is acquired

We sleep a few hours
Get up take a shower
Find food that we devour
All while watching Power

We change the sheets
Everything nice and neat
We aren't ready for sleep
We pull out the lighter, strike and repeat

The Dual Sides of My Gemini Mind

Doubt

He says he's laying down
And my mind starts to wonder
Is he in bed alone?
Or is there someone he's snuggled under

I can't do this to myself
Live in constant doubt
I need confirmation
That I'm not the only one holding out

He always wants me to confirm
I'm saving my love for him
He says that he belongs to only me
My past makes it hard to trust him

It also doesn't help
That this is long distance
And I can't have him next to me
The visits are too inconsistent

I haven't felt this way
In a very long time

LaRhonda N. Felton

I don't want him with anyone else
I need him to be all mine

I never planned to fall so fast
I had planned to take things slow
He has this charming ability
Keeps me wanting more
So again, he says he's laying down
Saying he's tired and needs to rest
Wish I was there to keep him warm
And I could fall asleep on his chest

Time's Up

He's begging me to stay
Pleading and talking
I'm packing my clothes
Bullshit and lies got me walking

I can't even look at him
I told him from the start
Don't fuck me over
Don't break my heart

What does he do?
Laugh it off and lie
Now he's looking stupid
I'm too mad to cry

I'm not that needy chick
Always checking her man
Stalking and calling
Going through his pants
I let him be a grown up
Handle his shit

LaRhonda N. Felton

He thought I was a fool
Tried to be slick

That's where he fucked up
Bruh, who you fooling?
When I walk out
Like a baby, you will be crying and drooling
I'm the best thing you ever had
I know that for a fact
When everyone left you hanging
I had your back

Not anymore
Your ass is on your own
I may be single
But I won't be alone
Even your boy has tried to holla
But I'm not that low
Won't give him shit to go on
Y'all won't be comparing notes
But this is your loss
You fucked up, jackass
I no longer give a damn
You're now part of my past

The Dual Sides of My Gemini Mind

Got to be More Careful

He said he didn't feel well
So, I picked him up some soup
Pulling up to his house
I see his basketball on the stoop
I knock on the door
And it's slightly ajar
I call his name
He can't be too far

This place is a mess
Dishes everywhere
I call his name again
Is he even here?
I make my way down the hall
I hear voices slow and low
Maybe he's on the phone
Which explains the open door

I approach his bedroom
I hear music in the background
Low moans and giggles
I can see candles melting down

LaRhonda N. Felton

This can't be real
I don't believe what I see
He's making love to her
Right in front of me
I drop the soup
She grabs the cover
I look right into his eyes
Dirty motherfucker

He jumps up
I turn to leave
He's trying to explain
This, I can't believe

He's screaming, "I don't love her
Baby please, listen"
I'm looking for my keys
All understanding is missing

I turn and I slap him
Hard across the face
If I could find my keys
I would spray his ass with mace
The tears burn the back of my eyes

The Dual Sides of My Gemini Mind

As they start to fall
Who can help me?
Who the hell can I call?

I scream and yell
"Help me find my keys!"
I must get out of here
Is this trick trying to leave?
He's in my way
Trying to block my view
I look around him
Bitch, don't I know you?

I remember, she works with me
And she knew he had a girl
But she doesn't owe me shit
It was him that promised me the world

I look at him again
And I hate him for this
He's saying it was nothing
His lies I merely dismiss

My stomach is in knots

LaRhonda N. Felton

And suddenly I feel sick
I race to the bathroom
Before I puke all over his shit
I see my keys
On the floor near the soup
I grab them on my way out
He's now out on the stoop

"Baby please
It's not how it seems"
I kick his basketball
Into the middle of the street

"You can't be serious
You told me you were sick
All so you could cheat on me
With that random bitch"

"Baby listen to me
You know I love you
I don't want her
Let me make it up, boo"

The Dual Sides of My Gemini Mind

"Make it up?
Have you lost your fucking mind?
I need to get in my car
Before I end up doing time
Here I am
Thinking you're sick
And you, on the sheets I bought
Fucking that dirty bitch
Hear me good, fuck all of this
And double fuck you
Fuck that nasty ass tramp
And this relationship too!"

"Baby, can you calm down?
At least let me explain"

"You can talk all you want
It won't erase my pain
I'm walking away
From your trifling ass
Lose my fucking number"

I'm in my car foot on the gas
Three weeks later

LaRhonda N. Felton

I'm still sick as hell
And I've skipped a period
A few more minutes and time will tell

As I wait on the results
Of this pregnancy test
I pray it's negative
I can't handle any more stress
My alarm beeps
I don't make a sound
Please let it be negative
I fall to the ground

Yet again, the result is positive
For the fifth time in a row
I must face the fact
There's now a baby in tow
I pick up my phone
This is truly fucking sad
This cheating ass liar
Is my new baby's dad

Tears fall again
Soaking my face

The Dual Sides of My Gemini Mind

My love for him is gone
Never to be replaced
I dial his number
He answers right away
I let him know
The events of my day

I will make an appointment
To be undeniably sure
But from this heartbreak he caused
There is no cure

We can co-parent
And that's about it
What did I ever do
To deserve this shit?

LaRhonda N. Felton

The Dual Sides of My Gemini Mind

Prioritize

So, you left the door open
I'm walking through
What else would you
Expect me to do?

You made it clear
Wanted me to see
That in your life
I'm no longer a priority

You left me longing
And very unfulfilled
Leaving me to find someone
That will seal the deal

Since you left me guessing
On what would be your next move
Don't be surprised when I cater
To the one that shows and proves

You left me alone
Because you don't make the time

LaRhonda N. Felton

Expect me to reciprocate love
To the one that can't keep me off his mind

When you lose me
And I'm a part of your past
You won't have a right to be upset
You made your bed, you should be glad

The Dual Sides of My Gemini Mind

Slow Dance

Music playing
And he holds me tight
Our hearts sync up
And everything feels right

I smell his skin
And it takes my breath away
We both move to the beat
While his hands are around my waist

Old school R&B
I remember all the words
He's singing in my ear
So low, he can barely be heard

The feel of his breath in my ear
Sends tingles down my spine
I feel the shift in his energy
Nostalgia sets in, reminding me of other times

That our song has been played
And the two of us hit the floor

LaRhonda N. Felton

Dancing so close together
People don't do this anymore

Which is why I adore him
He still makes the effort
To show me I'm special
Over the years, it's only gotten better
We all need to be shown
Love and adoration
He makes sure I feel his love
Without any hesitation

And at this old house party
He takes this chance
To show me even more love
With a romantic slow dance

The Dual Sides of My Gemini Mind

His Boys

I'm doing the laundry
And going through his pockets
A twenty here and a fifty there
He really needs to stop it

I've told him more than once
Hence, the reason for a wallet
Money all over
In damn near every pocket

His jeans felt heavy
In those pockets I go
What the fuck?
Oh, hell no

What is he doing?
What's going on?
Why am I holding
A brand-new gun

I don't make a move
I scream his name

LaRhonda N. Felton

He has a shocked look on his face
He says, "Let me explain"

I place my hands on my hips
A blank stare on my face
"Well, get to the point
Don't make me wait"
He begins to talk about the other night
Out with his boys
And some misunderstanding
And he had to hush all that noise

Now down this road
We've been before
I did this bid with you
When they slammed the prison door
Six long years
Of praying and waiting
Lonely nights
You constantly stating
That you would change
Things wouldn't be the same
And now that you're home
You talking to me like I'm some lame

The Dual Sides of My Gemini Mind

Those boys of yours
Don't mean shit
You weren't gone two good weeks
Before a couple of them tried to hit

They knew your ass would be gone
Caught yourself a bid
They still came around
Pretending they were just checking in

So, don't come stalling and stuttering
Like I'm slow
I made it very clear to you
I wouldn't do this anymore
So, if this is the life you want
Please let it be known
I will pack my shit quick
And get the hell on

He is looking super stupid
You better say something quick
His mouth is wide open
Help me understand this shit

LaRhonda N. Felton

Baby, I'm sorry
It won't happen again
But what do you want me to do?
Make new friends?

You're a grown ass man
I expect better choices
You need to silence them so called friends
Hang out with men and not boys
They're hyping you up
On some real dumb shit
Meanwhile, their hands are clean
You catch another charge, looking stupid

Baby forgive me
It won't happen again
I promise this time
Am I forgiven?

I shake my head
And roll my eyes
You need to get it together
'Cause I am surely tired

The Dual Sides of My Gemini Mind

Baby I'm making you a promise
I won't go back on my word
I owe you my life
You are my world
But I do need to know
The names of those friends you meant
That came back when I left
Trying to hit

Are you serious?
Is that all you heard?
Let me get out of here
This conversation is absurd

Baby wait, no don't leave…
I need to leave because this is a joke
You're taking this too lightly
And that gives me no hope

Do you know what I went through when you left?
Picking up the pieces
Taking care of you as well as myself
You made these promises
And not a month after you're free

LaRhonda N. Felton

You're being led by them
Fuck this, I must protect me
Wait just a minute
Let me prove I meant what I said
I need you in my life
Baby, don't make me beg

You get one more chance
Or I pack my shit
And I won't have to worry
If you're truly legit
But I will say this
And hear me well
I won't argue next time
I refuse to live in hell
I will simply walk away
Your words won't win
Be very mindful
Because the ice you're on is thin

Baby I hear you
And I give you my word
This is the last time
I refuse to lose my girl

The Dual Sides of My Gemini Mind

I will make you proud
And soon you will see
I will restore your faith
In us and in me

I love you more than anything
I'm done with the streets
Let me show you I'm serious
Take another chance with me

I'm following my heart
And I'm deciding to stay
But fuck up once more
And I will not hesitate
You and I will be over
No ifs, ands, or buts
You have one more chance
You better not fuck this up

LaRhonda N. Felton

The Dual Sides of My Gemini Mind

Girls' Night Out

Slipping into my freak-um dress
Girls' night out is always the best
We laugh and flirt
Do our little dirt
We get a party bus
To chauffeur all eight of us
Drinks fill our cups
We get lit and turn up

Our bond is tight
We love as hard as we fight
We talk about life, love and our men
Sipping vodka, rum and gin

We laugh and we cry
Because we truly care
And when one of us is in need,
We're all there

Others have come along
And tried to infiltrate
But there's no drama here,

LaRhonda N. Felton

We can always spot a snake

On the bus, shoes come off
And some eyelashes too
When we're together,
There's no telling what we'll do

I love these girls
And I know they love me
We push each other
To pursue our dreams

Our circle is tight
And our bond is strong
We converse and laugh
All night long

We ride around the city
All of us looking sexy and pretty
We never hit the clubs despite
That is the sole purpose of girls' night

The Dual Sides of My Gemini Mind

Gemini

Expressive
Twins
Dual personality
Play to win
Conversationalist
Natural flirt
Life of the party
Extroverts
Emotional
Quick-witted
Air sign
Pretty
Curious
Romantic
Serious
Manic
Misunderstood
Very creative
Loving
Relishes misbehaving
Laughter
Sadness

LaRhonda N. Felton

Bordering on

Madness

Moody

Petty

Do me wrong?

I won't forget it

Giving

Perceptive

Thoughtful

Reflective

Forgiving

Honest

This is all me

I promise

Sexy

Naughty

Humble

Haughty

Protector

Sensitive

Does anyone know?

Only if I mention it

A small look inside

The Dual Sides of My Gemini Mind

Words used to describe
The dual sides
Of my Gemini mind

LaRhonda N. Felton

About the Author

Although Author LaRhonda N. Felton's love for writing was recognized and nurtured early, she often struggled with taming the habit of censorship. Even after winning second place in a short story contest in 8th grade and later having one of her poems published in a national anthology, it took more time to fully acknowledge her undying passion for the craft.

With a myriad of life experiences to draw from, LaRhonda's forward-thinking ideas on love and life soon began to pour out at an uncontrollable rate. A self-proclaimed realist who is admired by most for her honesty, she learned how to simply let the words flow, no longer concerned about who the truth may offend. This unrestricted freedom of expression allowed her to discover a personal niche, strictly focusing on the erotic aspects of adulthood.

The Dual Sides of My Gemini Mind is her second published collection of poetry. *In The Meantime* was her first, and she has many other manuscripts on standby.

www.ingramcontent.com/pod-product-compliance
Lightning Source LLC
Chambersburg PA
CBHW070603010526
44118CB00012B/1438